AWESOME PASSOVER COLORING BOOK

THIS BOOK BELONGS TO

....

COLOR TEST PAGE

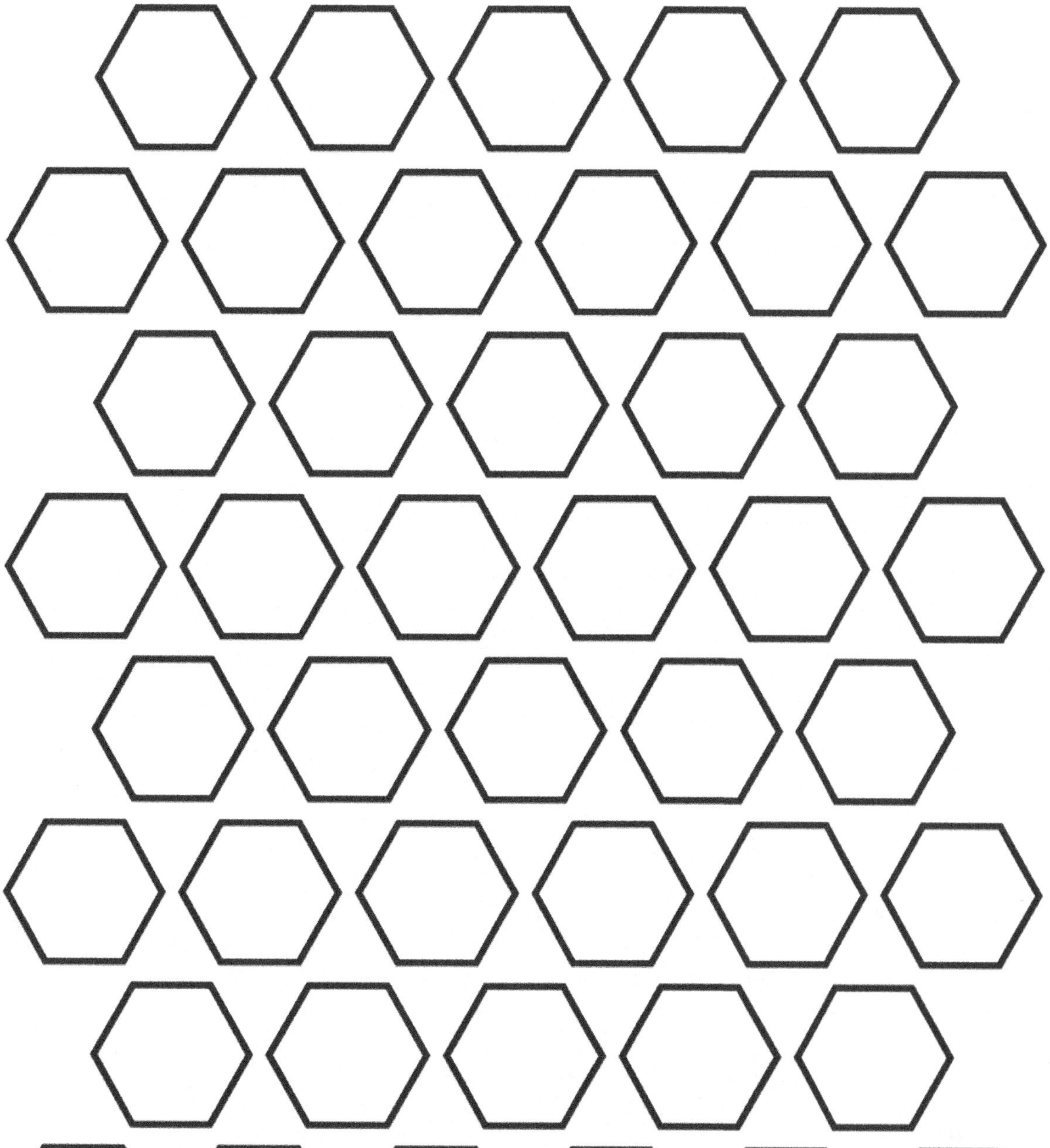

NOTE FROM THE PUBLISHER

THANK YOU FOR CHOOSING US.

WE HOPE YOU HAVE A GREAT COLORING
EXPERIENCE WITH THIS BOOK

WOULD YOU WRITE US A REVIEW!!
IT TAKES ONLY FEW SECONDS

THERE IS NO OBLIGATION
BUT ALL REVIEWS ARE APPRECIATED.
WE LOVE HEARING FROM OUR CUSTOMERS
AND IT HELPS US DO A GREAT JOB

THANKS FOR BEING AWESOME

ENJOY

זרוע

חזרת

פסח

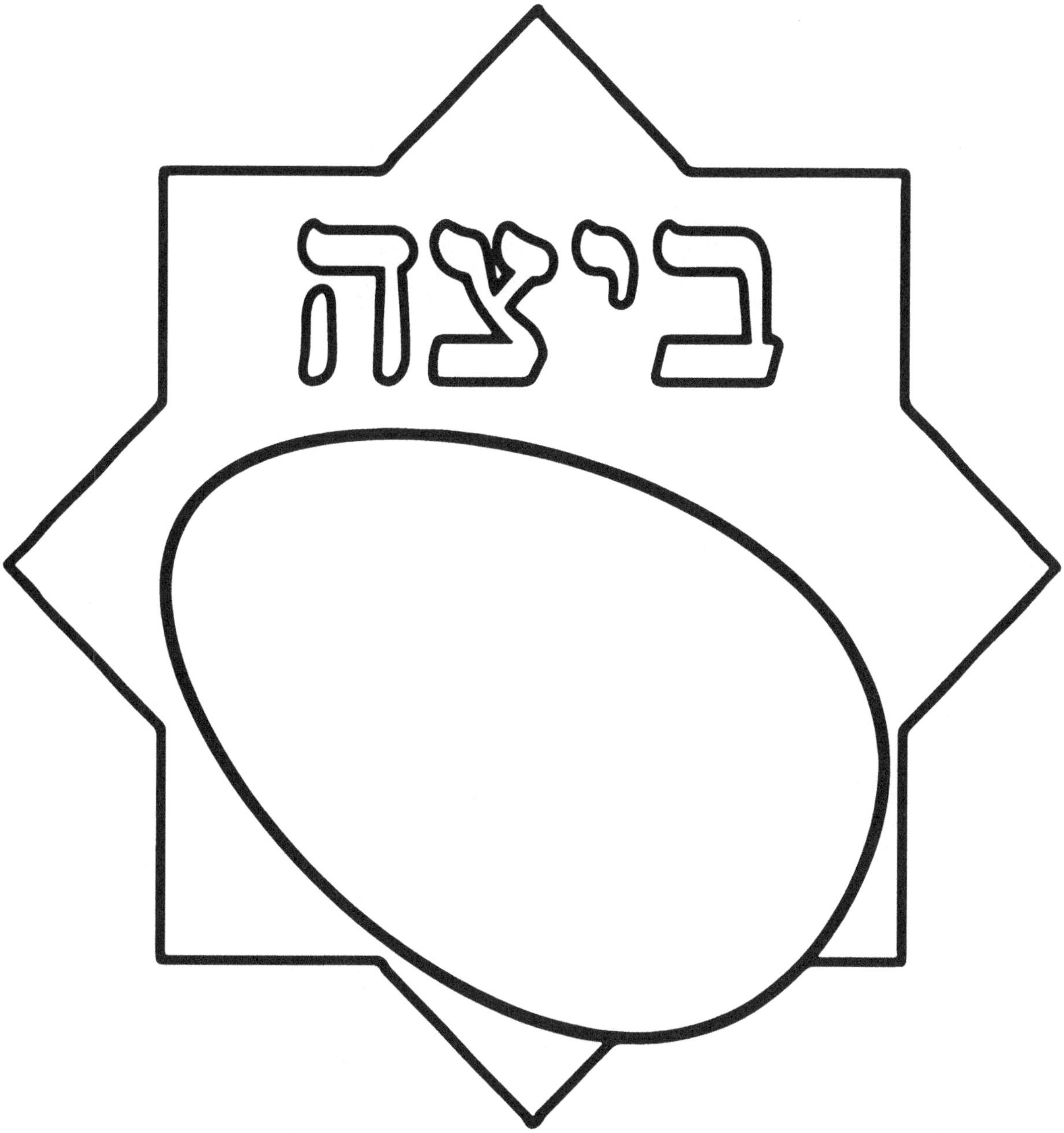
ביצה

נורור

errrr

NEXT YEAR IN JERUSALEM

I
II
III
IV
V
VI
VII
VIII
IX
X

HAGGADAH FOR PASSOVER

PaSSOVER

Made in the USA
Monee, IL
08 April 2024

56619789R00057